HOLI HINDU FESTIVAL OF SPRING

Olivia Bennett

Photographs by Christopher Cormack

Evans Brothers Limited

'Hello! I'm Manisha. I live in Coventry. Today our school is celebrating the arrival of Spring. It is so cold I think Spring has forgotten to come this year. I can't wait to get into the warm classroom.'

Today is also the day when Hindus everywhere celebrate their own festival of Spring, called Holi. Some of the pupils will be performing Indian dances. These retell two of the stories which are retold every year during Holi.

Manisha is making an elephant mask for a dancer. She carefully cuts out the head with its big ears. Abbas cuts out the trunk.

'That's right, Abbas, Put a few blobs of glue there.'
Miss Stransky helps them glue the trunk onto the elephant's face. She has designed all the costumes for the dances. This mask is for one of the boys taking part in the story of Prahlad and his wicked father King Hiranyakashup.

Asiya, Manisha and Abbas have great fun painting the mask. Manisha puts blue dots around the eyes. In India, elephants sometimes parade through the streets during festivals. They wear beautiful head-dresses of bright colours with tiny shiny mirrors sewn into the material.

At two o'clock, everyone crowds into the school hall to watch the dances. Mrs Chatterjee taught the children the Holi dances. She explains how, all over India, stories are told through dancing. The people love this kind of storytelling.

'India is a huge country. Each region has its own special ways of celebrating Holi. One of the most popular is by retelling the story of Prahlad. It reminds us why many Hindus celebrate Holi by lighting a bonfire. Our second story is about Krishna, the child god, and his friend Radha. It tells us why people throw coloured powders at Holi.'

'Watch the dancers' hands. They tell us what is going on. This hand movement means Krishna is playing his magic flute.'

'Radha's friends carried pots of water on their heads like this.'

The first dance begins with Prahlad saying his prayers. Prahlad believed in God. His father, King Hiranyakashup, did not. He wanted Prahlad to treat him as God. Prahlad knew this was wrong and he refused. So the wicked King tried to kill him. He ordered his soldiers to throw Prahlad into a big pit full of poisonous snakes. Many snakes bit Prahlad but he was saved from death by God.

Then the King sent a troop of big elephants to trample all over Prahlad while he slept. Once again, God protected Prahlad from harm.

The King refused to give up. He tried other ways of killing Prahlad.
Each time he failed. Finally he asked for help from his wicked sister Holika.
Holika had a special gift. Fire could not harm her. So she took Prahlad to the
top of a huge bonfire. She thought she would be safe and Prahlad would be
burnt to death.

Girls in flame-coloured skirts dance in and surround Prahlad.
They wave their arms to show the hot flames leaping up around him.

Suddenly they bow down quietly. Prahlad steps out of the fire unharmed.
God has protected him. Holika's magic power is broken and she disappears
in the flames. This is why many Hindus light bonfires at Holi. It reminds them
of how God saved Prahlad and how goodness won over evil.

The second dance tells the story of how, many years ago, Krishna and Radha started the festival of Holi.

It is a beautiful evening in India. Krishna is playing his magic flute. His friends are dancing by the banks of the River Yamuna and enjoying the lovely spring weather.

Krishna playfully throws some coloured water at a beautiful girl called Radha. Soon everyone is laughing and throwing colours at each other. Nobody minds the mess. They have had a wonderful time.

Ever since then people in India have celebrated Holi by throwing coloured powder, paint and water at each other. Everyone dresses up in their old clothes. Then it doesn't matter how messy they get!

The dancers can't throw coloured water or powders in the school hall.
So they throw pretty coloured papers instead. Soon the dancers and the
floor are covered in red, yellow, green and blue confetti.

The music comes to an end. Everyone claps. Manisha hurries home.
She finds her cousins Krishna and Paresh playing outside.
'Our families are going together to the temple to celebrate Holi,'
says Krishna.

Manisha quickly changes her clothes. Mum is making dough for
chapattis. While Manisha tells her about the dances at school, Mum rolls out
the mixture of flour and water into flat circles. Damiyanti, another cousin,
is washing up.

Manisha's aunt cooks the chappatis over the gas flame. The bread turns brown and puffs out.

Mum says, 'I've got some more cooking to do. Why don't you and Damiyanti go off to the temple now? We'll follow later.'

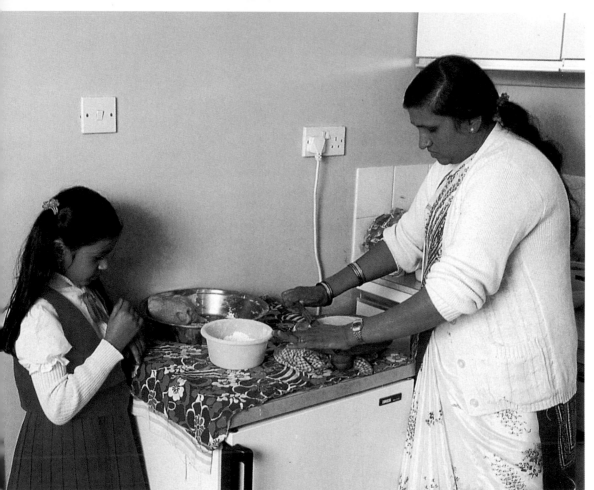

Manisha and Damiyanti walk through the cold streets to the temple. Strings of coloured lights twinkle outside the building. A huge pile of wood stands in the courtyard.

It is warm and peaceful inside the temple. Damiyanti and Manisha take off their shoes and enter the prayer hall. They walk around the three shrines, saying prayers. The main shrine has a picture of Radha and Krishna.

The priest puts offerings of flowers and fruit in front of the shrines.
The prayer hall begins to fill with people. Manisha's grandmother
arrives. She rings the temple bell softly.

After some prayers she sits down with the other worshippers. Everyone has been waiting for her because she sings so well. She begins a song of praise to God. People join in the gentle singing and clapping.

The priest lights some small oil lamps. The bright flame reminds people of the presence of God.

People pass their hands over the flame and then over their head.
Manisha calls this 'taking some of God's spirit'. It helps people feel
closer to God.

The priest asks Damiyanti to take the holy flame to all the women.
Then he offers everyone some special food, called prasad. This has been
blessed and offered to God.

The temple grounds are overflowing with people. It is time to light the bonfire. The priest says some prayers. Holy water is poured onto the wood. Then the bonfire is set alight.

'God will protect us, just like he saved Prahlad. We can't be hurt by the flames,' whispers Manisha to Damiyanti. She clings tightly to her cousin's hand, afraid to lose her in the crowd.

The flames start to leap up to the sky. People throw in sweet dates, popcorn, rice and even money. The women walk around the fire. They pray that their children will be as happy and healthy as Krishna was when he was a baby.

They pour holy water onto coconuts and fling them into the flames.

Most of the coconuts are then pulled out. The hairy outer skin is a little charred. The coconut is broken into pieces. The milk is poured out and the delicious white flesh shared by family and friends. Everyone remembers how good overcame evil in the story of Prahlad. They feel happy.

The bonfire starts blazing fiercely. Sparks shoot into the sky.
Faces glow in the flamelight. Small children sit on their parents'
shoulders so that they can see what is going on.
'My face and hands are warm now,' says Manisha, 'but my feet are still cold.'

Damiyanti takes Manisha home. The street outside the temple
is full of people and cars. A bright red fire engine stands by in case
the fire gets too big!

24

When the family get back, they tuck into the delicious food that Mum has cooked for Holi.

Before Manisha goes to bed she shares the last of the prasad with Krishna. The priest gave it to her mother to bring home. The cousins agree that the best parts of Holi were the storytelling and the bonfire.